Bibliographic information published by the German National Library:

The German National Library lists this publication in the National Bibliography; detailed bibliographic data are available on the Internet at http://dnb.dnb.de .

Imprint:

Copyright © 2017 GRIN Verlag, Open Publishing GmbH
Print and binding: Books on Demand GmbH, Norderstedt Germany
ISBN: 9783668519633

This book at GRIN:

http://www.grin.com/en/e-book/373474/data-mining-to-business-analytics-finance-budgeting-and-investments

Jagdish Chandra Patni, Ravi Tomar, Hitesh Kumar Sharma

Data Mining to Business Analytics. Finance, Budgeting and Investments

An Evolutionary Approach

GRIN Publishing

GRIN - Your knowledge has value

Since its foundation in 1998, GRIN has specialized in publishing academic texts by students, college teachers and other academics as e-book and printed book. The website www.grin.com is an ideal platform for presenting term papers, final papers, scientific essays, dissertations and specialist books.

Visit us on the internet:

http://www.grin.com/

http://www.facebook.com/grincom

http://www.twitter.com/grin_com

Abstract

With the increment of monetary globalization and development of information technology, financial data are being produced and gathered at an extraordinary pace. Thus, there has been a basic requirement for automated ways to deal with compelling and proficient usage of gigantic measure of data to support companies and people in doing the Business. In our project we expect to utilize the distinctive mining techniques as an answer for business needs. It presents **Finance, Budgeting and Investments** as the principle working ground for the data mining algorithms actualized.

Data mining is turning out to be strategically imperative region for some business associations including financial sector. Data mining helps the companies to search for hidden example in a gathering and find obscure relationship in the data. Financial Analysis alludes to the assessment of a business to manage the arranging, budgeting, observing, forecasting, and enhancing of every financial point of interest inside of an association. Our task concentrates on comprehension the association's financial health as a major part of reacting to today's inexorably stringent financial reporting prerequisites. It exhibits the capacity of the data mining to robotize the procedure of looking the boundless customer's connected data to discover patterns that are great indicators of the practices of the customer. This will cover the analysis of: Profit arranging, Cash flow analysis, Investment decisions and risk analysis, Dividend Policies and Portfolio Analysis through algorithms like Apriori, Naivebayes, Prediction algorithm and so forth. Along these lines this Data mining arrangement actualizes advanced data analysis techniques utilized by companies for discovering startling patterns extricated from tremendous measures of data, patterns that offer applicable knowledge for anticipating future results. The undertaking gives a thought of how data mining abilities can give the expanded customer maintenance and minimizes the risk included in the financial sectors to accomplish upper hand and finishes up by giving the constraints and opportunities in this field.

Table of contents

1. Introduction

In this modern era, we tend to trust that data prompts force and accomplishment, because of fashionable advancements, for instance, PCs, satellites, and then forth, we've got been gathering mammoth measures of knowledge. At first, with the approaching of PCs and means that for mass processed reposition, we tend to begin gathering and putt away a large vary of knowledge, looking on the force of PCs to agitate this amalgam of knowledge. Lamentably, these vast accumulations of knowledge place away on dissimilar structures quickly have to be compelled to be resistless. This beginning turmoil has prompted the formation of organized database systems. The skilled direction systems are essential resources for management of an in depth corpus associated notably for compelling and effective recovery of specific information from an expansive accumulation at no matter purpose needed. Today, we've got far more data than we are able to deal with: from business exchanges and investigatory data, to satellite photos to content reports and military information. Data recovery is simply inadequate any further for alternative creating. Stood up to with monumental accumulations of Knowledge we have got currently created new must provide USA some help with creating higher choices. These wants reprogrammable summarized data, extraction of the importance of knowledge place away, and also the revelation of examples in crude data. With the large live of knowledge place away in documents, databases, and totally different stores, it's more and more essential, if a trifle a lot of, to grow intense means that for investigation and perhaps translation of such data and for the extraction of intriguing learning that might facilitate in alternative creating.

1.1.   Data Mining- An Introduction

In the 21st century individuals are utilized as a part of distinctive innovations to sufficient the general public. Every last day individuals are utilizing the immense information and these information are from different fields. It might be as archives, may be graphical formats, possibly the video, and perhaps records (fluctuating arrays). As the information are accessible in the diverse formats so that the correct move to be made. To examine these information as well as take a decent choice and keep up the information .When the client requires the information ought to get recovered and settle on good choice .The system is called as an Data mining or the KDD(Knowledge Discovery Process).

Data mining, the extraction of the hidden prognosticative knowledge from substantial databases, may be capable new innovation with extraordinary potential to supply organizations some help with specialising in the foremost important knowledge in their knowledge distribution centres. Data processing tools foresee future trends and practices, allowing businesses to create proactive, info

4

driven selections. The mechanized, close at hand analyses offered by data processing move past the analyses of past occasions gave by review tools regular of call showing emotion subsidiary networks. Data processing tools will answer business addresses that typically were tedious, creating it not possible to be seen. They scour databases for hidden patterns, finding prognosticative knowledge that specialists might miss in lightweight of the actual fact that it lies outside their needs. Most organizations effectively gather and refine vast amounts of information. Data processing methods is actualised quickly on existing programming and instrumented stages to upgrade the good thing about existing knowledge assets, and maybe incorporated with new insights and frameworks as they are brought online. The live of crude knowledge place away in company databases is blasting. From trillions of purpose of-offer transactions and MasterCard buys to pixel-by-pixel photos of worlds, databases area unit presently measured in gigabytes and terabytes. (One T = one trillion bytes. A&T inadequate around a pair of million books!) For case, each day, Wal-Mart transfers twenty million purpose of-offer transactions to an A&T vastly parallel framework with 483 processors running focused information. Crude knowledge while not anyone else, be that because it might, doesn't offer a lot of knowledge. In today's viciously targeted business surroundings, organizations got to quickly remodel these terabytes of crude knowledge into noteworthy bits of data into their purchasers and markets to manage their advertising, speculation, and administration procedures.

Data mining tools foresee practices and future trends, allowing businesses to form proactive, learning driven choices. Data processing tools will answer business addresses that usually were overly tedious, creating it not possible to work out. They scour databases for hidden patterns, findingprognosticative knowledge. Knowledge applying therefore on mine investigates the information a large assortment of procedures, created for the effective treatment of considerable volumes of information. The six essential data processing systems are exhibited underneath:

• **Classification:** Contains of a capability which maps (groups) a knowledge issue into one in all some predefined categories.

• **Regression**: Includes a capability which maps a knowledge issue to a real reputable prediction variable.

• **Clustering:** May be a typical clear trip wherever one appearance to tell apart a restricted arrangement of classifications or bunches to portray the information.

• **Association guideline learning (Dependency modeling):** Contains of discovering a model that portrays vast conditions between variables.

• **Anomaly detection (Change and deviation detection)**: Concentrates on finding the hugest changes within the knowledge from beforehand measured or regulation qualities.

• **Summarization:** Includes techniques for locating a reduced description for a set of information.

Data mining has developed within the previous twenty years, turning into a principal revelation method. It's consolidated techniques from varied totally different fields, as well as statistics, machine learning and information systems.

1.2. Business Analytics – Emerging Trends

Business analytics is that the act of unvaried, systematic discovery of an association's knowledge with accentuation on measurable examination. Business analytics is employed by organizations centered on data-driven deciding. The sphere of business analytics has increased altogether within the course of recent years, giving business purchasers higher bits of data, particularly from operational knowledge place away in transactional systems. The data sets created by inculcating records on single click created by internet web site activity with demographic and alternative behavioral data smaller person, in size and many-sided quality, the largest knowledge distribution centers of solely some of years previous. The result is mammoth databases requiring a mix of machine-controlled investigation techniques and human push to present business purchaser's strategic understanding concerning the activity on their sites, and additionally concerning the attributes of the sites' guests and customers. With various an excellent several clickstream records created on a daily basis, aggregative to client targeted records with many attributes. There's some clear demand for machine-controlled techniques for locating patterns within the knowledge. During this manner the innovation and venture choice trends related to business analytics seem.

1.3. Evolving Data Mining into Solution for Business Analytics

The key shopper is that the business shopper, whose occupation, conceivably in promoting, showcasing, or deals, isn't squarely known with analytics in essence, however rather World Health Organization normally utilizes exposition tools to reinforce the after effects of some business method on one or a lot of measurements, (for example, profit and time to advertise). Luckily, data processing, systematic applications, and business data systems are presently preferred incorporated with transactional systems over they once were, creating a shut circle within the middle of operations and

6

analysis that allows knowledge to be stony-broke down and therefore the outcomes mirrored chop-chop in business activities. Mined data these days is sent to a lot of in depth business gathering of individuals exploiting business analytics in its regular exercises. Analytics are presently habitually used as a locality of offers, advertising, inventory network improvement, and extortion detection.

Most associations gather knowledge concerning their operations. They then examine this knowledge for bits of information into their operations and into the transactions the business makes. This could be as basic as alluding a program, to examine the numbers for rational soundness, or it's going to embrace graphical Associate in nursing lysis with an OLAP instrument. However, manual analysis normally must stop as of at once — checking out evident basic connections. An automatic data processing methodology, however, will frequently discover productive connections we have a tendency to might not even have suspected existed, or that you just knew would take too long to find by manual suggests that. Machine-controlled data processing permits the event of models of spectacular complexity which might think about varied a lot of parts. Data processing has been used to acknowledge unforeseen searching patterns in grocery stores, Optimize web site gainfulness by creating fitting offers to each guest, Predict client reaction rates in advertising effort, Distinguish within the middle of productive and unfertile customers so on. Data processing could be characteristic development of the dilated utilization of mechanized knowledgebase to store data and provides answers to business examiners. Data mining is characterized as a business process for work lots of knowledge to search out necessary patterns and pointers. Organizations will apply data processing with a selected finish goal to reinforce their business and increase points of interest over the contenders. The foremost essential business territories that effectively apply data processing are:

1.**Retail:** Retail data processing will acknowledge client buying practices, notice client searching patterns and trends, enhance the character of client administration, accomplish higher client maintenance and satisfaction, improve product utilization proportions, style a lot of powerful merchandise transportation and distribution approaches, and reduce the expense of business.

2. **Banking:** There are totally different regions within which data processing is used as a locality of cash connected segments like client division and gainfulness, credit analysis, anticipating instalment default, marketing, pretend transactions, positioning ventures, upgrading stock portfolios, cash administration and prognostication operations, high risk loan candidates, most efficient MasterCard Customers and Cross marketing.

3. Insurance: Data processing can give insurance some help with firming in business practices, as an example, procuring new customers, holding existing customers, acting advanced classification or relationship between policy coming up with and policy selection.

Figure 1.Business areas that creatively utilise data mining (Source: Wikipedia)

Our application zone in this undertaking will be Finance, Investments and Budgeting. Finance associations are extricating new bits of data from existing and recently accessible interior wellsprings of knowledge, characterizing significant information innovation procedure and at the moment incrementally increasing the wellsprings of knowledge and foundations over the end of the day. Necessities of knowledge mining in finance area unit forthcoming from the necessity to: Predict dimensional time arrangement with abnormal state of clamor; Contain explicit fitness criteria (e.g., the best of commerce Profit) however prediction exactness, incorporate the blow of sector players on sector regularities. The enterprise can depict concerning distinctive data processing techniques used as a vicinity of economic information analysis. Money information analysis is employed as a vicinity of various money organizations for precise analysis of client information to get defaulter and substantial client. It will cover the analysis of: Profit arranging, Cash flow analysis, Investment decisions, risk analysis, Dividend Policies and Portfolio Analysis. Along these lines this Data mining arrangement execute propelled data analysis techniques utilized by companies for discovering startling patterns removed from immeasurable measures of data, patterns that offer applicable knowledge for anticipating future results.

2 .Related Work

2.1.   The Research and Implementation of Data Mining

With the wide utilization of business intelligence in corporate, the interest for data mining programming expands every day. To enhance the efficiency and nature of the reusing data mining programming and decrease the period and expense of creating data mining application framework, this paper proposes another part library arrangement of data mining. Through componentization of data mining calculation, this framework actualizes differed center calculations of data mining as parts. Along these lines, the efficiency and nature of creating data mining programming are enhanced altogether to meet different application requests.

2.2.   Use of Data Mining in Various Field

Data mining concentrates the knowledge from a lot of data which stores in various heterogeneous database. Information are passing on the message through immediate or circuitous. This paper gives a study of different data mining techniques. These techniques incorporate affiliation, relationship, bunching and neural system. This paper likewise leads a formal survey of the use of data mining, for example, the instruction part, marketing, fraud detection, assembling and telecommunication. It talks about the subject taking into account past explorations furthermore ponders the data mining techniques.

2.3.   Review of Various Data Mining Techniques

A lot of information place away in databases is increasing at a huge pace. This needs a demand for brand new techniques and tools to assist folks in naturally and brightly work large knowledge sets to obtain valuable data. This developing want provides a perspective for an additional analysis field known as data Discovery in Databases (KDD) or data processing, that pull during a thought from researchers during a wide selection of fields as well as info style, statistics, style acknowledgment, machine learning, and knowledge illustration. Data processing is that the procedure of discovering sagacious, intriguing, and novel patterns, and in addition partaking, affordable and prognostic models from large scale knowledge. This paper outlines numerous tasks incorporated into data processing. Data processing includes the tasks like anomaly detection, classification, regression, generalization and agglomeration.

2.4. Data Mining Solutions for the Business Environment

Data mining has become a matter of spectacular significance as a result of plenty of knowledge accessible within the applications having an area with completely different areas. Data processing, a dynamic and fast extending field, that applies advanced information analysis techniques, from statistics, machine learning, info systems or manmade learning ability, keeping in mind the tip goal to seek out necessary patterns, trends and relations contained inside the data, information for utilizing completely different techniques. This text concentrates on displaying the utilizations of knowledge mining within the business surroundings. It contains a general review of knowledge mining, giving that means of the thought and spoken language the elemental fields that data processing are often connected. It to boot shows the principle business ranges which might profit by the use of knowledge mining tools, aboard their utilization cases: retail, banking and insurance. Likewise the elemental industrially accessible data processing tools square measure displayed. Apart from the analysis of knowledge mining and also the business regions that may effectively apply it, it displays the first components of an information mining arrangement that may be connected for the business surroundings and also the design that will enhance client encounters and decision-production.

2.5. Applications of Data Mining Techniques in Banking Sector

Data mining is popping resolute be strategically imperative zone for a few business associations together with banking sector. It's a procedure of cutting down the information from completely different points of read and presses it into necessary information. Data processing helps the banks to go looking for hidden example in an exceedingly gathering and realize obscure relationship within the knowledge. Today, customers have such an oversized variety of feelings with relevance wherever they will do their business. Early knowledge analysis techniques were placed toward extricating quantitative and factual knowledge attributes. These techniques encourage valuable knowledge translations for the banking sector to stay removed from client sporting down. Client maintenance is that the most crucial variable to be analysed in today's targeted business surroundings. What is more fraud could be a noteworthy issue in banking sector. Distinctive and avoiding fraud is difficult, in lightweight of the very fact that fraudsters grow new plans perpetually, and therefore the plans develop additional advanced to flee easy detection. This paper analyses the info mining techniques and its applications in banking sector like fraud dodging and detection, client maintenance, selling and risk management.

2.6. A Detailed Review on Data Mining in Finance Sector

Financial data is utilized as a part of numerous financial foundations for exact assessment of customer's data to discover account holder and legitimate consumer. This data be equipped for be put away and kept up to deliver information and truths. This information and knowledge must be flowed to each partners for the powerful decision making procedure. Because of the upgrade in the data, it is huge to mine information from vast data stores. Subsequently, Data mining is turning into a critical component in different fields including business, education, and healthcare, finance, logical and so forth. This paper tells about data mining and its techniques utilized as a part of financial sector.

2.7. Study Financial Data Analysis through Data Mining Techniques

This paper depicts concerning various data processing techniques used as an area of monetary knowledge analysis. Financial data knowledge analysis is employed as an area of diverse monetary institutions for precise analysis of shopper knowledge to find defaulter and valid client. For this various data processing techniques are often used. The knowledge consequently got are often used for higher cognitive process, This paper offers insights concerning loan default risk analysis, variety of evaluation and various data processing techniques like Thomas Bayes classification, Boosting, call Tree, Random forest algorithmic program and numerous different techniques.

2.8. Data Mining in Banking Sector

The industry has full-fledged completely different changes within the method they direct the business and spotlight on leading edge innovations to contend the sector. The banking business has begun understanding the importance of creating the cognitive content and its use for the benefits of the bank within the zone of strategic desperate to create due within the centered sector. Within the leading edge time, the advances are advanced and it encourages forming, catching and storing knowledge dilated vastly. Knowledge is that the most profitable quality, significantly in finance industrial enterprises. The estimation of this quality are often assessed simply if the association will disencumber the necessary data hidden in crude knowledge. The increment within the large volume of information as a chunk of everyday operations and thru different inward and external sources, strengths info innovation industrial ventures to utilize advances like data processing to vary data from knowledge. Data processing innovation offers the workplace to urge to the proper info at the proper time from tremendous volumes of crude knowledge. Banking industrial enterprises receive the data mining advances in numerous regions significantly in client division and profit, Predictions on costs of distinctive speculation merchandise, currency market business, dishonorable dealing detections, risk predictions, default prediction on estimating. Its profitable device that acknowledges conceivably useful info from vast live of information from the association will devour an affordable purpose of interest over its rivals. The study from this paper demonstrates the criticality of information mining innovations and its points of interest within the banking and finance sectors.

3. Background

Dramatic advances in knowledge capture, process power, knowledge transmission, and capability skills square measure empowering associations to coordinate their totally different knowledge base into data warehouses. Knowledge Disposition is characterized as a procedure of targeted knowledge management and recovery. Knowledge deposition, the same as data processing, could be a usually new term in spite of the actual fact that the thought itself has been around for quite a durable. Knowledge deposition speaks to an ideal vision of maintaining a focal storage of all hierarchical knowledge. Centralization of knowledge is anticipated to reinforce shopper access and analysis. Sensational innovative advances square measure creating this vision a reality for a few firms. What is a lot of even as emotional advances in knowledge analysis programming square measuring allowing customers to urge to the present knowledge? Knowledge warehouses square measure used to unite knowledge set in divergent databases. Information warehouse stores substantial amounts of knowledge by specific classes therefore it is all a lot of effortlessly recovered, translated, and sorted by purchasers. Warehouses empower directors and chiefs to figure with unfathomable stores of transactional or different knowledge to react speedier to business sectors and choose a lot of educated business choices. It's been anticipated that every business can have a data warehouse inside 10 years. In any case, solely swing away knowledge in an exceedingly knowledge warehouse will a corporation stripped-down nice. Firms can have to be compelled to soak up a lot of this knowledge to boost information of shoppers and markets. The organization blessings once vital trends and patterns square measure aloof from the info.

3.1. Data Mining Foundations

Data mining techniques area unit the consequence of a protracted procedure of analysis and item development. This development started once business knowledge was ab initio place away on computers, proceeded with changes in knowledge access, and every one the a lot of as lately, created innovations that let purchasers to explore through their knowledge unendingly. Data processing takes this organic process past review knowledge access and navigation to planned and proactive info conveyance. Data processing is ready for application within the business cluster in lightweight of the very fact that it's bolstered by 3 advances that area unit presently adequately develop:

• Massive Knowledge Assortment

• Powerful digital computer computers

• Data mining algorithms

Business databases area unit developing at extraordinary rates. The going with demand for increased process motors will currently be met during a cost-successful means with parallel digital computer technology. Within the advancement from business knowledge to business info, every new step has based mostly upon the past one. as an example, dynamic knowledge access is basic for drill-through in knowledge navigation applications, and therefore the capability to store immense databases is basic to data processing. From the client's perspective, the four stages recorded in Table 1 were progressive in lightweight of the very fact that they permissible new business inquiries to be addressed exactly and quickly.

Table 1 Data Mining Evolution steps (Source: http://www.thearling.com/text/dmwhite/dmwhite.htm)

Evolutionary Step	Business Question	Enabling Technologies	Product Providers	Characteristics
Data Collection (1960s)	"What was my total revenue in the last five years?"	Computers, tapes, disks	IBM, CDC	Retrospective, static data delivery
Data Access (1980s)	"What were unit sales in New England last March?"	Relational databases (RDBMS), Structured Query Language (SQL), ODBC	Oracle, Sybase, Informix, IBM, Microsoft	Retrospective, dynamic data delivery at record level
Data Warehousing & Decision Support (1990s)	"What were unit sales in New England last March? Drill down to Boston."	On-line analytic processing (OLAP), multidimensional databases, data warehouses	Pilot, Comshare, Arbor, Cognos, Microstrategy	Retrospective, dynamic data delivery at multiple levels
Data Mining (Emerging Today)	"What's likely to happen to Boston unit sales next month? Why?"	Advanced algorithms, multiprocessor computers, massive databases	Pilot, Lockheed, IBM, SGI, numerous startups (nascent industry)	Prospective, proactive information delivery

The centre components of knowledge mining technology are being worked on for a substantial length of your time, in analysis zones, as an example statistics, processing reasoning, and machine learning. Today, the event of those techniques, plus superior social information motors and expansive knowledge integration endeavours, build these innovations useful for current knowledge warehouse environments.

3.2. Scope of Data Mining

Data mining gets its name from the similitudes between looking down vital business info during huge information - as an example, finding connected merchandise in gigabytes of knowledge and mining depression for a vein of vital metal. Each procedure needs either filtering through a vast live of fabric, or with wisdom testing it to find exactly wherever the price lives. Given databases of adequate size and quality, information providing thus on mine technology will produce new business opportunities these abilities:

14

• **Automated prediction of trends and practices.** Data processing computerizes the procedure of discovering prophetical information of vast databases. Queries that usually needed broad active analysis will currently be addressed specifically from the information very quickly. A commonplace illustration of a prophetical issue is concentrated on promoting. Data processing uses information on past special mailings to tell apart the objectives well on the thanks to augment degree of profitableness in future mailings. Alternative prophetical problems incorporate prediction financial condition and differing kinds of default, and recognizing fragments of a people susceptible to react likewise to given occasions.

• **Automated speech act of beforehand inconsistent patterns.** Data processing tools undergo completely different databases and acknowledge existing hidden patterns in one stage. A sample of example revelation is that the analysis of retail deals information to acknowledge apparently inconsequential merchandise that square measure often brought along.

3.3. Working of Data Mining

How is data processing able to allow us to grasp very important things that we have a tendency to did not grasp or what's planning to happen next? That strategy that's utilized to perform these accomplishments is named modeling. Modeling is largely the demonstration of building a model (an arrangement of cases or a scientific relationship) in lightweight information from circumstances wherever the solution is understood and afterwards applying the model to totally different circumstances once we don't know the answers. It's even as recently that knowledge warehousing and correspondence capacities needed to collect and store vast measures of information, and therefore the process power to mechanize modeling techniques to figure foursquare on the information are accessible. Once the model is fancied it will then be utilized as a region of comparable circumstances wherever we do not have the foggiest plan concerning the solution. As an example, say that we have a tendency to square measure the chief of selling for a telecommunications organization and we'd prefer to get some new long separation phone customers. We have a tendency to might simply haphazardly quit and mail coupons to the all-encompassing community -just about as we have a tendency to might haphazardly cruise the oceans looking for submerged fortune. In neither one in every of the cases would we have a tendency to accomplish the outcomes we have a tendency to wanted and clearly we've got the possibility to indicate improvement over random. Because the selling executive we've got entry to a substantial live of data concerning the larger a part of our customers: their age, sex, credit history and long separation line utilization. The ascent news is that we have a tendency to likewise have an excellent deal of data concerning our planned customers: their age, sex, credit history then forth. War issue is that we do not have the foggiest plan concerning the long separation line utilization of those prospects (since they're all told chance currently customers of our opposition). We'd prefer to concentrate on those prospects UN agency have lots of long separation utilization. We will fulfill this by building a model. Table 2 delineates the info utilized for building a model for brand new client.

Table 2 Prospecting Data Mining (Source: http://www.thearling.com/text/dmwhite/dmwhite.htm

	Customers	Prospects
General information (e.g. demographic data)	Known	Known
Proprietary information (e.g. customer transactions)	Known	Target

Mining the consequences of a test market speaking to an expansive yet moderately little specimen of prospects can give an establishment to distinguishing great prospects in the general business sector. Table 3 depicts a normal situation for building models: as to what will happen in future.

Table 3 Data mining to do Predictions (Source: http://www.thearling.com/text/dmwhite/dmwhite.htm)

	Yesterday	Today	Tomorrow
Static information and current plans (e.g. demographic data, marketing plans)	Known	Known	Known
Dynamic information (e.g. customer transactions)	Known	Known	Target

16

The analytical techniques used as part of data mining are regularly understood numerical algorithms as well as techniques. New feature is the utilization of these techniques for general business issues which are expanded by availability of data, economical storage and the processing power.

3.4.   Tasks of Data Mining

The data mining tasks are of numerous kinds. Relying upon the employment of knowledge mining result the info mining tasks are named:

• **Exploratory knowledge Analysis**: Within the archives incomprehensible live of information's are accessible. This data processing trip can fill the wants while not the data for what the client is seeking then It examine the information. These techniques are intelligent and visual to the client.

• **Descriptive Modeling:** It portray all the info, it incorporates models for general chance distribution of the info, assignation of the p-dimensional house into gatherings and models depiction the connections among the variables.

• **Predictive Modeling:** This model permits the estimation of 1 variable to be anticipated from the acknowledged values of various variables.

• **Discovering Patterns and Rules:** This enterprise is largely accustomed find the hidden example and to search out the instance within the bunch. In an exceedingly bunch numerous patterns of numerous size and teams are accessible.

• **Retrieval by Content:** The essential target of this enterprise is to get the info sets of as usually as attainable used as an area of the sound/video and extra footage.

17

3.5.   Data Mining System Types

Data mining systems may be classified as per the various criteria the classification has even as follows:

• **Classification of knowledge mining systems in line with the type of information supply mined:** In association of a huge live of data's square measure accessible wherever we've to order these data however these square measure accessible the bigger a part of times during a comparative manner. We've to rearrange these knowledge in line with its kind (maybe audio/video, content organization then forth).

• **Classification of knowledge mining systems in line with the info model:** There square measure such a range of variety of information mining models (Relational data model, Object Model, Object orientated knowledge Model) accessible and each last model we have a tendency to square measure utilizing the various knowledge .According to these knowledge show the info mining framework order the info within the model.

• **Classification of information mining systems in line with the type of data found:** This classification in lightweight of the type of data found or data processing functionalities, as an example, characterization, discrimination, classification, clustering, and so on. Many systems have a bent to be complete systems providing many data processing functionalities along.

• **Classification of information mining systems in line with mining techniques utilized:** This classification is in line with the info analysis methodology utilized, as an example, machine learning, neural systems, hereditary algorithms, statistics, mental image, info orientated or knowledge warehouse-oriented, then forth.

3.6. Life Cycle of Data Mining

The life cycle of an information mining venture contains of six phases. The succession of the phases isn't inflexible. Moving forward and backward between distinctive phases is continually needed. It depends on upon the results of each section. The phases are:

i.   **Business Understanding:** This section concentrates on comprehension the task objectives and requirements from a business purpose of read, then dynamic over this data into an information mining issue definition and a propaedeutic arrangement designed to accomplish the objectives.

ii. **Information Understanding:** It begins with a starting information assortment, to induce at home with the information, to acknowledge information quality problems, to seek out initial bits information into the information or to spot fascinating subsets to border theories for hidden information.

iii. **Information Preparation:** during this stage, it gathers all the distinctive information sets and build the assortments of the exercises basing on the start crude information.

iv. **Modeling:** during this section, totally different modeling techniques area unit chosen and connected and their parameters area unit adjusted to ideal values.

v.   **Evaluation:** during this stage the model is altogether assessed and looked into. The strides dead to create the model to make sure it fitly accomplishes the business objectives. Toward the top of this section, a call on the use of the information mining results need to be return to.

vi. **vi. Deployment:** The motivation behind the model is to create data of the information, the data picked up ought to be sorted out and exhibited in an exceedingly manner that the client will utilize it. The readying section may be as simple as making a report or as incredible as actualizing a repeatable data processing procedure across the endeavor.

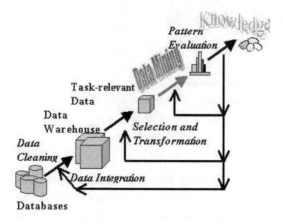

Figure 2 Data Mining as the Knowledge Discovery Process (Source: Author's own work)

3.7. Data Mining Methods

Some of the commonly used data mining measures generally classified as: Clustering, On-Line Analytical process, Classification, Generalization, Association, Temporal data processing, abstraction Mining and net Mining etc. These ways use varied kinds of algorithms and knowledge. Information supply will be file data warehouse, information or computer file. The algorithms are also applied with math's algorithms, Supported Vector Tree or Nearest Neighbor, supported Neural Network, supported Genetic Algorithms, Rules based mostly, Support Vector Machine etc. usually the info mining algorithms square measure seen to be utterly dependent of the two factors that are:

(i)   which sort of information sets we tend to mistreat

(ii)   what measure the sort of needs of the user

3.8 Data Mining Applications

- Future Conclusions of Health Care System
- Data mining for market basket analysis
- Data mining used to determine emerging trends in education system
- Data mining in manufacturing engineering
- Data Mining in Web Education
- Data Mining techniques in CRM
- Intrusion Detection in Network
- Credit Scoring
- The Intelligence Agencies
- Data mining system for the Internal Revenue Service

4. Problem Definition

The technology normally alluded to as data mining as of now exists in at any rate superficial structure. Tragically, for business clients, the data mining group is as of now concentrating on refining the technology, without endeavouring to validate it in business applications. From a common point of view, who cares if some algorithm is a 5% change over the best data mining method on the off chance that it just works from a summon line interface on some supercomputer? On the off chance that it isn't effortlessly usable, it is unessential to most clients. To convey data mining technology under the control of business clients, a few changes from the present condition of the technology will be required. These progressions can be separated into three key ranges:

- A built-in comprehension of business issues
- Ease of utilization (in particular executive level)
- Integration with relational database products

A marketing programming item won't succeed on the off chance that it doesn't begin with a comprehension of true business issues. Eventually the move between the model and business arrangement will require an intensive comprehension of the marketplace to define the issue in a way that will influence a business. The capacity of a marketing application to make utilization of this information will figure out whether is really valuable to a business. In this manner, industry-particular quality included arrangement suppliers will most likely have an imperative spot in the field of database marketing. They ought to have the capacity to contribute vertical market particular formats and meta-data that will manage the database mining technology toward answers for the business issues. Once the business issue has been mulled over, the procedure and results should be passed on to the business individual who needs to settle on a decision. It can't be expected that the individual who settles on the decision will see how to function with a neural system model or how to decipher the outcomes from such a model. Easy to understand graphical client interfaces (GUIs) are a need. These GUIs must coordinate easily into the business client's general decision bolster (DSS) application environment. Marketing applications must be easily coordinated with standard relational database products. Business clients would prefer not to manage dumping a RDBMS as a level document or deciphering between diverse data positions. Marketing applications need to work with driving relational database interfaces so they can communicate specifically with the databases. At the point when an application identifies with a database, it will likely be in SQL which is the standard for the database industry. Most of these things would be evident to designers of business programming, however not as a matter of course to those in the research oriented field of data mining.

In any association, directors need to take decisions while, arranging the exercises. By and large decisions were taken in light of past encounters, the style of working of the administrator and judgment. Then again, decisions taken in this way had the risk of settling on wrong decisions which would influence the cost of the venture. To beat this trouble supervisors have begun utilizing experimental techniques to assess the different options so that legitimate decisions can be taken. Decision making is a necessity in business and as any issue gets to be confused with vast info data, the analysis gets to be troublesome and subsequently a viable utilization of deliberate methodology is required. In this way extraction of Knowledge through Data Mining for the advantage of Business is Essential for development and growth of the organisation.

5. Architecture

Information is presently hold on in databases data warehouse systems therefore if we tend to arrange associate information mining system that decouples or couples with databases and knowledge warehouse systems. This ends up in having to four completely different architectures of a data mining system as follows:

1. No-coupling: During this design, data mining system doesn't use any utility of an information or data warehouse system. A no-coupling data mining system recovers data from a selected data sources, as an example, record system, processes data utilizing real data mining algorithms and stores results into document system. The no coupling data mining design doesn't take any preferences of information or data warehouse that are currently very expert in looking for, golf shot away, accessing and convalescent data.

2. Loose Coupling: During this design data mining system utilizes information or data warehouse for data recovery. In loose coupling data mining design, data mining system recovers data from information or data warehouse, processes data utilizing data mining algorithms and stores the result in those systems. This design is primarily for memory-based data mining system that doesn't need high skillfulness and superior.

3. Semi-tight Coupling: In semi-tight coupling data mining design, next to connecting to information or data warehouse system, data mining system utilizes some parts of information or data warehouse systems to perform some data mining undertakings as well as sorting, indexing, accumulation and so on.

4. Tight Coupling: In tight coupling data mining design, information or data warehouse is controlled as associate data recovery element of data mining system utilizing incorporation. All of the parts of information or data warehouse are used to perform data mining assignments. This design offers system ability, elite and incorporated data. There are 3 levels within the tight-coupling data mining architecture:

i. Data layer is associate interface for all data sources. Data mining results are hold on in data layer therefore it is presented end-user in variety of reports or alternative style of illustration.

23

ii. Data Processing Application Layer is employed to recover data from information. At correct time the data is processed utilizing completely different data mining algorithms. **iii. Front-end layer** offers natural and friendly computer program for end-user to attach with datamining system. Data mining result displayed in perception structure to the user within the front-end layer.

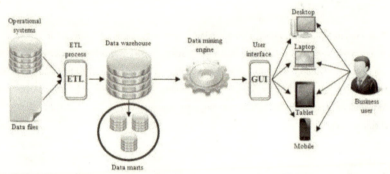

Fig. 3 Business Data Mining Architecture (Source: http://www.zentut.com/data-mining/data-mining-architecture/)

To best apply the propelled techniques, they need to be utterly coordinated with associate degree data warehouse and additionally versatile intelligent business examination tools. Various data mining tool set this time work outside of the warehouse, requiring extra strides for extracting, importing, and breaking down the data. Moreover, once new bits of information need operational implementation, coordination with the warehouse simplifies the appliance of results from data mining. The following analytic data warehouse will be connected to boost business processes throughout the association, in regions, as an example, special battle management, fraud detection, new product rollout, et cetera. Figure 4 delineates associate degree design for innovative examination in associate degree expansive data warehouse.

24

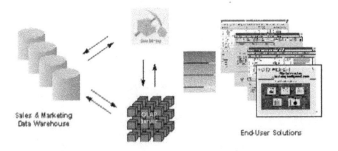

Sales & Marketing
Data Warehouse

OLAP
Server

End-User Solutions

Figure 4 Integrated Data Mining Architecture (http://www.thearling.com/text/dmwhite/dmwhite.htm)

5.1.   Essentials of Data Mining in Finance Sector

Essentials of data mining in the finance are returning from the requirement to:

- Prediction of **dimensional statistic** with high levels of noise;
- Contain specific ability criteria in supplement to prediction's accuracy like R2;
- Create coordinated **multi-tire** resolution forecast;
- Incorporation of a **stream of text signals** as input file for various prediction models
- To make a case for the **forecast** and prediction model ("black box" models have very little interest and future for important investment decisions);
- To get pleasure from **delicate patterns** with a brief life time;
- Integrate the erosion of market players on market regularities

25

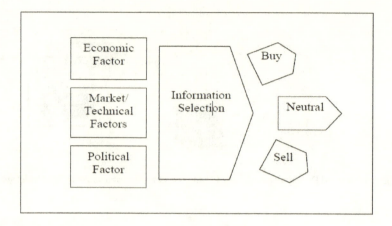

Figure 5 Cost of financial assets and the related Information (Source: Author's own work)

5.2. Setup of Three Tier Architecture

Generally an information mining application embraces a three-tier architecture. Setup of Client-Server Environment: GUI for User to connect with the application that will permit user to pick the information sets on which the algorithms must be connected. It has a user interface, which permits the user to choose and present the different sets of data over which information mining has to be performed. The pre and post-processing of information is dealt with by two modules to be specific, Association standard module and Rule impelling module. Mining for association administers fundamentally includes, discovering thing sets that happen with high recurrence and after that creating principles in light of these outcomes. For principle incitement CRITIKAL utilizes the idea of Contingency tables.

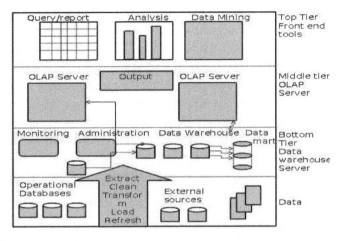

Figure 6 Three Tiers of the Data Mining Application Architecture (https://www.tutorialspoint.com/dwh/dwh_architecture.htm)

The second tier is the Data Mining engine architecture which is the genuine soul of the system. It is totally decoupled from the presentation layer, however its inside structure demonstrates a solid closeness with the one of the compartment GUI:

- There are some global services accessible to each specific information mining engine;
- There is a general reference unique model of the engine (a calculated structure);
- There are particular implementations of the genuine engines in light of the kind of information mining investigation to perform.
- The global services are utilized by each engine implementation, and are identified with: metadata management, configuration sparing/restoring, information access and DB connection management, inside information exchange and intersystem correspondence, information reduction.

Data warehouse or DBMS is the last Tier or Back end of a Data Mining Application. It comprises of the sorts of information that are collectively stored.

Business exchanges- Every exchange within the business is "memorized" for interminability. Such exchanges are usually time connected and might be between business arrangements, for instance, buys, exchanges, banking, stock, and so on., or intra-business operations, for instance, management of in-house wares and assets. Next is that the scientific info - whether or not during a Swiss nuclear accelerator center together with particles, or the Canadian woods concentrating on readings from a mountain bear radio neck.

27

Tragically, we will catch and store a lot of new info faster than we will examine the previous info formally gathered. Restorative and individual information- From government analysis to figure force and shopper records, substantial accumulations of data are unendingly assembled concerning people and gatherings. Governments, corporations and associations, are warehousing crucial amounts of individual info to supply them some help with managing human resources, higher comprehend a market, or essentially facilitate people. The World Wide internet repositories-Documents of a large vary of arrangements, substance and depiction are gathered and interconnected with hyperlinks creating it the most important store of data ever made. However it's dynamic and unstructured nature, its heterogeneous trademark, and it's all the time repetition and irregularity, the **World Wide Web** is that the most significant operation overtimes utilized for reference in lightweight of the wide assortment of subjects secured and therefore the vast commitments of resources and distributer.

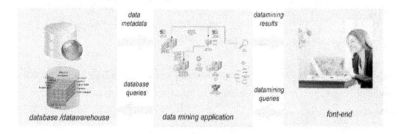

Figure 7 Description of Data Mining Application Workflow (Source: https://www2.microstrategy.com)

6. Algorithm

The algorithms which are applicable to the financial sector are explained in this section. Cash Flow Analysis plays a vital role in the finance sector. Preventing fraud is healthier than police work the fallacious dealing once its prevalence. Therefore for risk management, the info mining techniques call Tree, Support Vector Machine and additionally provision Regression etc. are used. Clustering model enforced victimization EM algorithmic can often be seen to sight fraud within the finance sector.

28

6.1. Bayes Classification

A Bayes classifier may be a basic probabilistic classifier in lightweight of applying Bayes' hypothesis with solid freelance assumptions and is particularly suited once the spatial property of the inputs is high. A naive Bayes classifier expect that the presence (or nonexistence) of a selected element of a category is random to the presence (or nonexistence) of no matter different part. Classification may be a sort of data investigation which might be used to concentrate models depiction essential data categories. Classification predicts all out labels (or separate values).Data classification may be a 2 stage method. Within the initial step, a model is assembled depiction a predestinate set of data categories or ideas. The model is developed by dissecting information tuples pictured by attributes. To start with, the discerning accuracy of the model is evaluated. The exactness of a model on a given take a look at set is that the rate of take a look at set examples that are effectively organized by the model. On the off likelihood that the accuracy of the model is viewed as worthy, the model is often used to order future data tuples or objects that the category mark isn't known.

1. Order the nodes according to their correct order.
2. Initiate importance function Pr(X\E), the required number of samples m and the value of updating interval is 1, and the score arrays is generated for every node.
3. k<-0 and T<-Ø
4. for i <-1 upto m, do
5. if (i mod 1 == 0) then
6. k <-k+1
7. update the importance function Prk (X\E) based on the value of T, end if
8. s$ <-generate a sample as per Prk (X\E)
9. T <-T U {si}
10. Calculate Score(si, Pr(X\E,e), Prk(X|E) and add this to the related entry of every array according to their instantiated states
11. Normalize the score arrays for each and every node. The major drawback of this model is that the predictive accuracy is highly correlated with its assumption.

6.2. Decision Trees

A decision tree could be a graph of choices and their dependable conceivable consequences. Highest hub during this tree is that the root hub on that a choice ought to be taken. In every inner hub, it's done as a take a look at on associate attribute or information variable. Significantly each branch of the tree could be a classification question, additionally the leaves of that tree are segments of the dataset with their corresponding classification. These algorithms take a goose the least bit conceivable identifying queries that might separate the primary making ready dataset into segments that are virtually solid as for the distinctive categories being anticipated. The restriction of this model is that, it cannot be summed up into a designed structure for all contexts. Decision tree could be a mapping from perceptions around an issue to decision concerning its objective value as a discerning model in data mining and machine learning. In these tree structures, the leaf nodes speak to classifications, the inner nodes speak to the present discerning attributes and branches speak to conjunctions of attributions that prompt the last classifications. The distinguished call trees algorithms incorporate ID3, C4.5 that is associate extension of ID3 algorithmic program and CART.

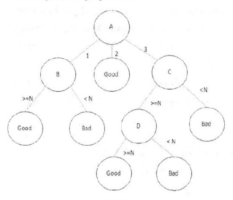

Figure 8 Structure of Decision Tree (Source: Wikipedia)

6.3. K-means Algorithm

It is an easy repetitious technique for partitioning a given dataset into a user specified variety of clusters, k. The algorithmic program works on a collection of d-dimensional vectors, $D = 1,..., N$}, wherever $xi \in$ second denotes the ith variety datum. The algorithmic program must be explicit by choosing k points in second because of the member of initial k cluster centroids. Techniques for choosing these initial seeds embody sampling haphazardly from the dataset, setting them as a remedy of agglomeration a little set of knowledge of the worldwide mean of the info k times. Then the algorithmic program must do:

Step 1: Data Assignment. Each datum is allotted to the closest center of mass, with ties broken abstractly. This results into the partitioning of knowledge.

30

Step 2: Relocation of "means". Each cluster whose representative is allotted to the middle (mean) of all knowledge points allotted thereto. If the info points square {measure} returning with the likelihood measure i.e. weights, then the relocation is to the expectations that square measure weighted mean of the info partitions.

Each iteration desires N × k comparisons that determines the time quality of 1 iteration. The amount of iterations that square measure needed for the convergence varies and will depend upon N, however as a primary cut, this algorithmic program might or might not be thought-about as linear in its dataset size. a problem to resolve this can be the way to quantify "closest" within the assignment step. One will simply show the non-negative worth of the cost operate in default value is that the geometrician distance, it'll have a decrease whenever there's some modification within the allocation steps, and hence the convergence are bonded solely with a relentless variety of iterations. The greedy nature of k-means on conjointly suggests that the convergence is merely to some native optimum. The algorithmic program is afterwards slightly sensitive to the initial center of mass positions.

6.4.   Apriori Algorithm

One of the foremost notable data processing approaches is to search out frequent itemsets derived from some transaction's dataset and so get the association rules from it. Looking out frequent itemsets aren't trivial attributable to the explosion. Thereby when the frequent itemsets are derived, it's easy to administer the association rules confidently on top of or up to a user fixed minimum confidence price. Apriori may be a seminal formula to search out frequent itemsets with use of candidate generation. It's represented that if AN item set isn't frequent, none of its superset will ever be frequent.

Let us assume the set of frequent itemsets of size k be the Fk and their corresponding candidates be Ck. It's seen that Apriori 1st scans the information and it then starts checking out frequent itemsets having the scale of one by aggregation the quantity of count for each item and accumulating those that abide by the minimum support demand. It then will the iteration for the subsequent three steps and extracts all of its frequent itemsets:

1. Generate $Ck+1$, the candidates of frequent item sets having the size $k+1$, from the frequent itemsets of size k.

2. **Scan the database**, calculate the support of all the candidates of frequent itemsets.

3. **Add** these itemsets which satisfy the minimum support requirement to $Fk+1$.

It generates $Ck+1$ from Fk by Generating $RK+1$, the starting candidates of frequent itemsets of size $k+1$ by taking the union of resultant two frequent itemsets having size k, Pk and Qk that have the first $k-1$ elements in common.

$RK+1 = Pk \cup Qk = \{iteml, \ldots, itemk-1, i\ temk, i\ temk\}$;

$Pk = \{i\ teml, i\ tem2, \ldots, i\ temk-1, i\ temk\}$;

$Qk = \{i\ teml, i\ tem2, \ldots, i\ temk-1, i\ temk\}$;

where it is seen that $iteml < i\ tem2 < \cdots < i\ temk < i\ temk$.

And next in the Prune step: Check whether all the itemsets of size k in $Rk+1$ are frequent and generate $Ck+1$ by removing those that do not pass this requirement from $Rk+1$. The reason is because any subset of size k of $Ck+1$ which is not frequent can never be a subset of the frequent item set having size $k+1$. Apriori, then, calculates frequency only for those candidates resulted this way by scanning the database. It is prominent that Apriori scans the database at most $k$max+1 times when the maximum permissible size of frequent itemsets has been set at k max. The Apriori has good performance by minimizing the size of candidate sets.

Figure 8 Apriori Algorithm (Source Wikipedia)

6.5. Support Vector Machines

In recent machine learning applications, support vector machines (SVM) are thought-about A must attempt because it delivers one among the foremost strong and correct ways among all well-known algorithms. It a sound theoretical foundation, desires simply a dozen examples for coaching, and is insensitive to the amount of dimensions. Also, economical ways to coach SVM are being developed at a quicker pace. During a two-class learning task, the target of SVM is to look the most effective classification operate to differentiate between members of the 2 categories within the coaching information. The metrics that the conception of higher classification operate needs to be realized. For linearly severable dataset, classification operate are going to be equivalent to a separated hyperplane f (x) that passes from the center of 2 categories. Once this operate has been determined, new data's instance xn needs to be classified by merely having to check the sign of theoperate f (xn); wherever it is derived that xn belongs to at least one of the positive class if solely f (xn) > zero. Since there are several of them such linear hyperplanes, what SVM afterward guarantees is that the most effective such operate is to be discovered by increasing the margin between the two categories. So the margin is outlined because the quantity of area, or partition between the 2 categories as outlined by the hyperplane. Speaking geometrically the margin relates itself to the shortest distance between the closest information purposes to some point on the hyperplane. It then permits United States of America to explore the way to maximize the margin so although there are associate degree infinite variety of hyperplanes, solely a number of qualify as an answer to SVM.

7. Implementation

7.1. Development Details

7.1.1. User Interface:

➢ Download and Install NETBEANS IDE.
➢ Create a new project BUSINESS-ANALYTICS.
➢ Select design pane and using Swing Functions design text boxes, panel, onclick buttons etc.
➢ Choose appropriate background image.
➢ Connect the buttons with the appropriate data mining algorithms written in java files.

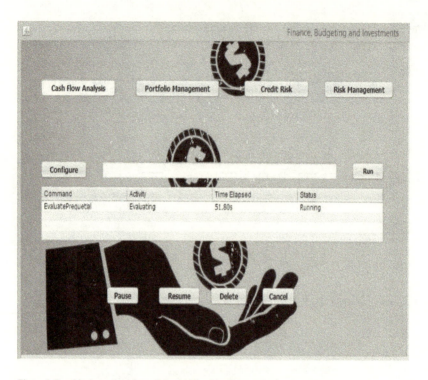

Figure 9 Graphical user interface of the Application (Source: Author's own work)

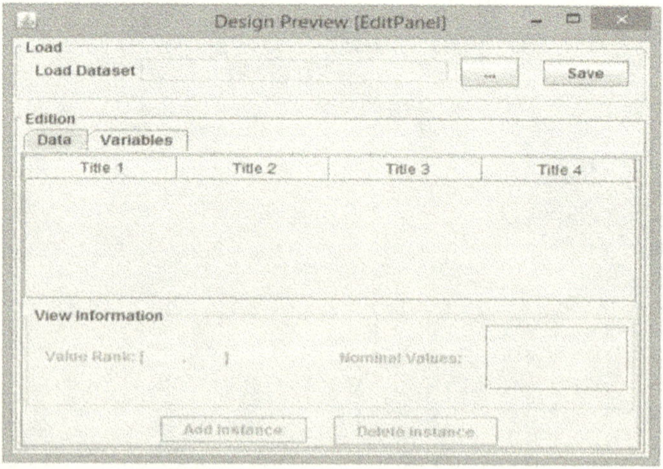

Figure 10 Data edit panel of the Application (Source: Author's own work)

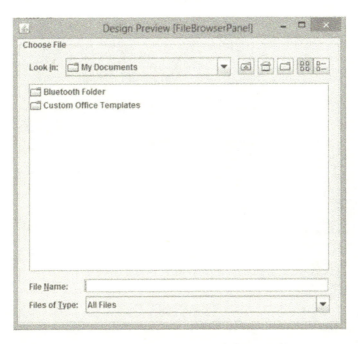

Figure 11 File browser panel of the Application (Source: Author's own work)

7.1.2. Source Code Configuration

➢ Configure any open source data mining tool in NetBeans or import java files from a jar file into the IDE. Example Weka, Orange, Apache Mahout, etc.

➢ Choose the java files containing the algorithms for different data mining techniques such as classification, clustering, generalization, prediction, summarization, regression according to the objectives.

➢ Copy these java files and import to BUSINESS_ANALYTICS and change the member variables and create classes wherever required.

➢ Import the classes wherever needed and remove the unused imports. Make all the necessary functions public in the java files so as to communicate in different packages.

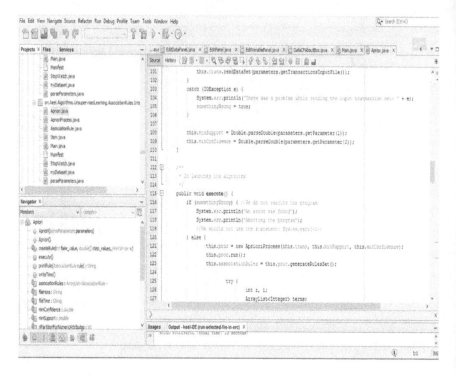

Figure 12 Netbeans Open Source Configuration (Source: Author's own work)

7.1.3. Algorithms Encoded

➢ The java files containing the algorithms for different data mining techniques now can be used independently on the data sets.

➢ These independent java files will be tested by running on the test sets prepared for different algorithms

➢ On successful completion of test, these files will now be kept away in different packages as per the algorithms contained in it .

➢ Make packages in the main project. Packages are – Associations; Classifiers; Clusterer; Regression; Prediction; Decision tree etc.

➢ Categorize the java files according to the techniques used in the algorithms and then copy them in their respective packages.

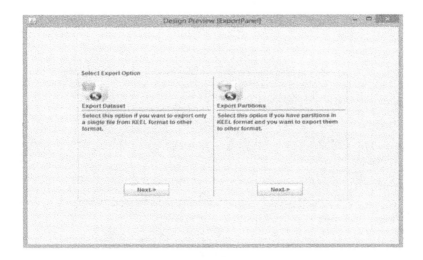

Figure 13 Export Files Panel of the Application (Source: Author's own work)

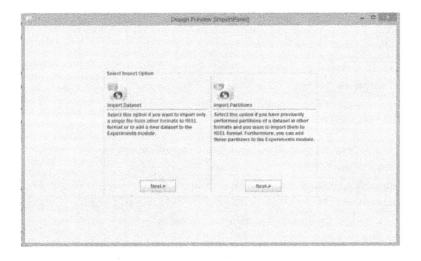

Figure 14 Import Files Panel of the Application (Source: Author's own work)

7.1.4.   Implementing Business Area- Finance, Budgeting and Investment

Data techniques and their respective algorithms have been chosen on the basis of their need in different fields in finance and investment sector.

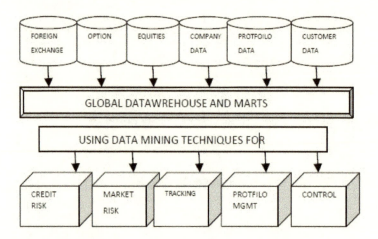

Figure 15 Financial business using Data Mining Technique (Source: Author's own work)

➢ **Cash Flow Analysis:**

Cash flow statement is one in all the foremost vital monetary statements for a task or business. The statement are often as basic as a 1 page analysis or might embody a number of schedules that encourage info into a focal statement. An income statement could be a posting of the flows of money into and out of the business or endeavour. Contemplate it you are monetary records at the bank. Stores square measure thought of because the money flow and checks square measure aforementioned to be the money outflows. The effort in your monetary records is your web income at a specific purpose in time. An income analysis enrols money flows that happened amid the past accounting part. The depiction of the longer term flows of money is thought as a income budget. It's not simply disturbed with the live of the money flows to boot the temporal order of the flows. Varied money flows square measure developed with completely different time sections. Example, it's going to list month to month money inflows and outflows over a year's time. It not simply activities the money parity staying

38

toward the top of the year to boot the money parity for each month. The technique that we tend to square measure capital punishment to try and do this is often Prediction strategy and decision tree.

• **Decision trees:** They are the foremost outstanding discerning models. a call tree could be a tree-like graph talking to the relationships between a collection of variables. Decision tree model are used to require care of the classification and forecast problems wherever examples are classified into one in all 2 categories, ordinarily positive and negative, or churner and non-churner within the churn classification case. These models square measure spoken to and evaluated in an exceedingly top-down means. Making decision trees includes 2 phases: Tree building and tree pruning. Tree building begins from the foundation hub that speaks to a feature of the cases that ought to be classified. Feature determination depends on assessment of the knowledge develop quantitative relation of every feature. Taking once constant method of data increase assessment, the lower level nodes square measure engineered by emulating the divide and conquer procedure. Building a decision tree consolidates 3 key components:

1. Identifying elements at the hub for cacophonic info as per its price on one variable or feature.
2. Identifying a stopping principle for selecting once a sub-tree is created.
3. Identifying a category result for each terminal leaf hub, as an example, _Churn' or _Non-churn'.

Decision trees usually prove to be immense if not cropped to find the most effective tree. The pruning method is employed to form a littler tree furthermore on guarantee a superior speculation. This method includes characteristic associate degreed evacuating the branches that contain the most important evaluated mistake rate and may be viewed as an experimentation method. The explanation for this method is to boost discerning accuracy and to cut back the decision tree quality.

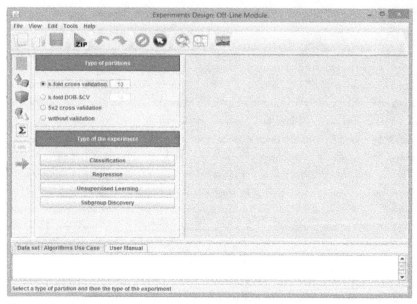

Figure 16 Experiment Panel of the Application (Source: Author's own work)

> **Risk Management**

Data mining methodology distinguishes borrowers who reimburse loans straight off from the people who do not. It to boot predicts once the receiver is at default, whether or not giving credit to a particular client can evoke awful loans then forth. Executives by utilizing data processing procedure will likewise break down the conduct and unwavering quality of the purchasers whereas giving credit cards additionally. It likewise breaks down whether or not the client can create provoke or defer instalment if the charge cards area unit oversubscribed to them. Finance Market Risk will be explained as: for the only financial instruments, i.e. stock records, interest rates, or currencies, market risk extent relies on models betting on a collection of basic risk component, as an example, interest rates, stock lists, or financial improvement. One is fascinated by a sensible assortment between instrument price or risk and hidden risk factors and to boot in helpful dependence of the chance factors itself. Nowadays various market risk estimation methodologies exist. Each one of them rely on models talking to single instrument, their conduct and interaction with general market. Massive parts of this should be created by utilizing completely different data processing techniques on the restrictive portfolio information, since information isn't freely accessible and wishes dependable management.

40

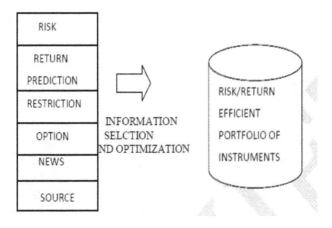

Figure 17 Instrument Portfolio (Source: Author's own work)

Method used is:

- **Value Prediction Methods:** During this methodology, as an example, rather than classifying new loan applications, it tries to predict expected default amounts for brand spanking new loan applications. The anticipated values are numeric and therefore it needs modelling techniques that may take numerical knowledge as target variables. Neural Network and Regression square measure used for this purpose. The foremost fashionable data processing strategies used for client identification are:

7.2. Association Rule Mining

> **Portfolio Management**

Risk estimation approaches on associate degree massed portfolio level live the chance of a group of instruments or client investigating enlargement effects. Then again, estimating models provides starting of the value of the financial tools. Each create it conceivable to superintend firm wide portfolio effectively in a very risk productive means. With the information mining and improvement methodology monetary specialists will assign capital crosswise over exchanging exercises to expand profit or minimize risk. Trademark bolsters the capability to come up with exchange suggestion and portfolio organizing from user equipped profit and risk essential. With data processing techniques it's conceivable to administer general circumstance examination capability with regard to expected plus costs or returns and also the risk enclosed. With this utility, imagine a state of affairs within which

41

recreations of adjusting market circumstance e.g. rate of interest and rate changes will be race to gauge sway on the worth and risk connected with portfolio, business unit counterparty, or exchanging work space. Totally different state of affairs results will be respect by take into account real market conditions. Profit associate degreed misfortune examinations allow user to spellbind a plus category, locals or sub-portfolio will be benchmarked against the common universal benchmarks. The technique used is:

- **The Clustering model:** Clusterisation helps in gathering the information into comparable clusters that aides in uncomplicated recovery of knowledge. Cluster analysis could be a methodology for breaking information down into connected elements in a very manner that patterns and request gets to be noticeable. This model relies on the employment of the parameters' information clustering areas. When classification, the stocks can be chosen from these gatherings for building a portfolio. It meets the paradigm of minimizing the chance by enlargement of a portfolio. The cluster methodology orders stocks on bound investment criterions. The results of our analysis demonstrates that the K-means cluster analysis fabricates the foremost conservative clusters for stock classification information. We tend to then choose stocks from the clusters to fabricate a portfolio, minimizing portfolio risk and so distinction returns and of the given benchmark file.

> **Credit Risk**

Credit risk analysis is vital part within the technique of business disposition. while not it the loaner would be unable create a target judgment of endure to lend to the planned receiver, or if the number of charge for the advance. Credit risk management may be classified into 2 elementary gatherings:

1. Credit scoring/credit rating. Assignment of a client or a product to risk level.
2. Behavior rating or credits migration analysis. Aggregation of a customer's or product's probability of adjustment in risk level inside a given time (i.e., default rate unpredictability)

In business disposition, risk appraisal is usually a trial to live the chance of misfortune to the loaner once creating an exacting disposition call. Here credit risk will enumerate by the progressions useful of a credit product or of a whole credit client portfolio that is predicated on amendment within the instrument's fuming, the default probability, and convalescence rate of the instrument if there ought tobe an incident of default.

Additional broadening effects power the end result on a portfolio level. Consequently a stimulating piece of implementation and thought of credit risk management system are going to be a run of the mill data processing issue: the modeling of the credit instrument's worth in the course of the default chances, rating migrations, and revival rates. 3 principal approaches exist to model credit risk on the exchange level: accounting analytic approaches, applied mathematics prediction and selection abstractive approaches. Since substantial live of knowledge regarding shopper exist in finance business, a satisfactory approach to amass such models is to utilize their own information and data processing techniques, fitting those models to the requirements of the business and current credit portfolio of business.

- **Regression Model:** it's supported supply regression, stepwise-logistic regression, multi criteria call creation technique and exponential pervasive beta 2 (EGB2) supply model could be a finished direct model that's used for binomial regression as a neighborhood of that the investigator variables may be in addition numerical or categorical. It's essentially accustomed lookout of problems caused by insurance and business fraud. A share of the examination has planned supply regression based mostly model to foresee the presence of economic statement fraud. Applied mathematics technique for supply regression will acknowledge impure monetary statements effectively. Likewise Neural Network is a good modeling instrument. It by and enormous offers most correct and pliable models. It's something however tough to make neural network prognosticative models. Network illustration tools can guide users from configuration, training, testing, and every one a lot of considerably direct application to databases. Regression produces numerical capacities for anticipating default risk levels. It may be exceptionally proscribing to be used as a universally helpful credit risk prognosticative modelling ways. But once it is used with huge than systems, it may be an exceptionally useful strategy.

7.3.1. Integration and Deployment Phase

➢ Connect the on-click buttons and text boxes on GUI with java files contained in different packages.
➢ User will choose the file from the system or URL from web in the textbox created in GUI.
➢ The data chosen must be ARFF format, or must be from end data warehouse.
➢ Now user has to choose the algorithm to be applied on the data set and set the output file.

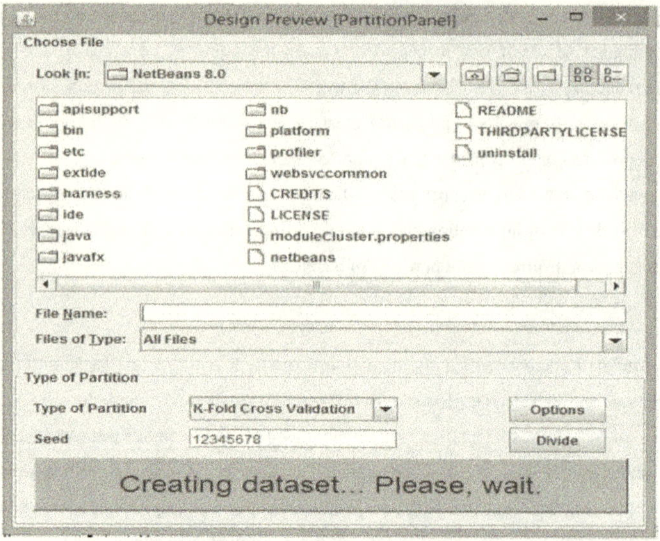

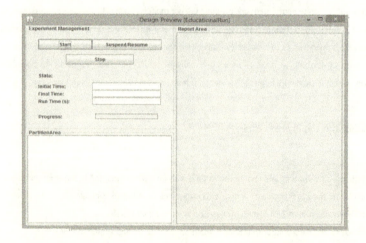

Figure 18 Partition Panel of the Application (Source: Author's own work)

Figure 19 Output Panel of the Application (Source: Author's own work)

8. Conclusion

Data Mining is an equipment of techniques accustomed separate vital data from the gathered knowledge, empowers finance institutions to decide on higher decision prediction method. Knowledge Collections are as maintaining legitimate deposition seeable of distinctive knowledge bases and different connected sources like documents into a worthy data cluster that turns into the data for data processing procedure. Seeable of the quality or rules set by the association and body powers, data processing device untangle the information in lightweight of the rule set and tosses the yield in visual tools, during this manner creating finish consumer life easy to decide on choices licitly. Banks and monetary associations began allocation subsidizes and time for corporal punishment data processing tools within the zone of call realizing therefore on build the requirement of information mining in their framework. data processing techniques will be of facilitate to the banks and monetary foundations during this structure for higher targeting and deed new customers, fraud detection in real time, loaning merchandise supported segmentation therefore on have higher targeting of the shoppers, conjointly analysis of the shoppers purchase patterns over time for higher retention, detection of rising trends to require a lively stance in an exceedingly extremely competitive market giving high price to the already existing merchandise and therefore the services so the launching of recent product and repair bundles.

Our project aimed to focus data mining application within the finance sector for extracting helpful information. The prediction of risks utilizing data processing applications could be attesting endeavor however it positively diminishes the human toil and builds the indicative exactitude. The info mining technology could completely have an effect on monetary sector. It's inferred that the capability to utilize data processing could be a very important criteria for a good institution. Moreover it's found that there's not a big association between the information of information mining and therefore the goal of tolerating data processing technology. Utilizing data processing advances as a section of monetary field can render an aggressive predominance for the business operations. The business operations that coordinate data processing techniques with their monetary foundation, that empowers estimation of future taking into consideration past knowledge, empowers the unconditional parties to form pre-emptive estimations and to make a decision the conceivable risks. Data processing techniques are exceptionally useful to the finance sector for higher specializing in and procuring new customers, most vital client maintenance, programmed credit endorsement that is used for fraud compensatory action, fraud detection endlessly, giving fragment based mostly merchandise, analysis of the shoppers, dealing patterns when your time for higher maintenance and relationship, risk management and promoting.

Data Mining Issues

Data mining algorithms include the techniques that are generally already existed for therefore a few years, however have solely recently been applied as a really reliable and a climbable tool that beat out older classical applied math strategies every time. Whereas data processing remains in its get-go, it's turning into a pattern and pervasive. Before data processing forms into a customary, develop and trusty management, various hitherto unfinished problems should be attended. A number of these problems are

Security and social issues: Security is an essential issue with any knowledge assortment that's shared and/or is projected to be utilized for strategic decision-production. Likewise once knowledge is gathered for client identification, consumer conduct comprehension, dealing individual knowledge with alternative information. Lots of delicate and personal info regarding folks or firms is accumulated and place away. This gets to be dubious given the classified approach of a number of this knowledge and also the potential unlawful access to the data. To boot, data processing may reveal new verifiable information regarding folks or gatherings that would be against security arrangements, notably if there's potential unfold of found information.

i.   **Interface issues:** The information found by data processing tools is efficacious the length of its fascinating or a lot of all excusable by the consumer. Good knowledge facilitates the interpretation of knowledge mining results, and conjointly offers shoppers some help with remedial comprehend everyone wants. Various knowledge alpha analysis tasks area unit altogether inspired by the capability to envision knowledge during an appropriate visual presentation.

ii. **Mining strategy problems:** These issues relate to the info mining methodologies connected and their impediments. Themes, as an example, flexibility of the mining methodologies, the various qualities of knowledge accessible, the spatiality of the world, the expansive analysis wants (when known), the appraisal of the information found, the misuse of foundation information and information, the management and treatment of commotion in knowledge, and then forth area unit all samples that may direct mining approach choices. As an example, it's often enticing to own various data processing routines accessible since distinctive methodologies could perform contrastingly looking forward to this knowledge. Besides, distinctive methodologies could suit Associate in Nursing justify client's needs in a sudden approach. Data processing techniques have to be compelled to have the capability to handle clamor in knowledge or fragmented info. Over the life of knowledge, the extent of the hunt area is way a lot of unequivocal for data processing techniques.

46

iii. **Performance issues:** Several counterfeit consciousness and measurable systems exist for knowledge analysis and elucidation. Be that because it could, these routines were often not designed for the massive knowledge sets data processing is managing these days. This raises the problems of ability and potency of data mining ways once process imposes vast data. Algorithms with exponential and even medium-request polynomial many-sided nature cannot be of handy use for data processing. Straight algorithms area unit usually the quality.

iv. **Knowledge supply problems:** There are various issues known with the info sources, some are right down to earth, as an example, the variations of knowledge types, whereas others are philosophical just like the knowledge excess issue. We have a tendency to unquestionably have Associate in Nursing abundance knowledge since we have a tendency to as of currently have a lot of knowledge than we can touch upon and that we are hitherto gathering data at a way higher rate. Within the event that unfold of direction systems has enlarged the social event of knowledge, the looks data mining is totally promising a lot of data gathering. Associate in Nursing variable data processing instrument, for a good vary of knowledge, might not be smart. Additionally, the proliferation of heterogeneous knowledge sources, at basic and linguistics levels, postures very important difficulties to database cluster still on the data mining cluster.

v.

8.1.   Future Scope of Data Mining

In an amount of short period, the results of information mining are thought to be in profitable, if mundane, business connected areas. Smaller scale promoting effort can investigate new specialties. Promoting can target potential customers with new accuracy. Within the medium term, data processing is also as traditional and straightforward to use as email. We tend to could utilize these tools to find the simplest transportation to London, deracinate a phone number of a departed cohort, or find the simplest costs on yard cutters. The long run prospects are genuinely energizing. Envision shrewd operators turned free on therapeutic analysis knowledge or on sub-nuclear molecule knowledge. Computers could uncover new medicines for sicknesses or new experiences into the means of the universe.

Because of the tremendous action of various application zones of information mining, the sector of information mining has been fitting itself because the vital management of computer code engineering and has indicated interest potential for the long run developments. Steady increasing technology and future application territories are reliably postures new difficulties and open doors for data processing, the run of the mill future trends of information mining incorporates:

i.   **Standardization of Data Mining dialects:** There are totally different data processing tools with numerous sentence structures, afterward it's to be institutionalized for creating advantageous of the shoppers. Data processing applications must pack a lot of in institutionalization of cooperation dialects and adjustable consumer communications.

ii.   **Knowledge pre-processing:** To acknowledge useful novel patterns in confiscated, vast, remarkable and worldly knowledge, data processing techniques must advance in numerous stages. The current techniques and algorithms of information pre-processing stage don't seem to be up to the imprint contrasted and its importance in deciding the novel patterns of information. In future there's an unbelievable want data mining applications having acceptable data pre-processing techniques.

iii. **Advanced objects of Knowledge:** Data processing goes to enter altogether fields of human life; the within the blink of a watch accessible data processing techniques are confined to mine the standard kinds of data simply, and in future there's a clear stage for data processing techniques for advanced knowledge objects like high dimensional, quick knowledge streams, grouping, clamor within the time arrangement, chart, Multi-occasion objects, Multi-spoke to things and transient knowledge.

iv.   **iv. Computing resources:** The up to date developments in quick network, parallel, conveyed, lattice and distributed computing has postured new difficulties for data processing. The quick net network has pictured an unbelievable interest for novel and effective data processing techniques to research the large knowledge that is caught of science parcels at high affiliation speeds therefore on acknowledge the Denial of Service (DoS) and differing types of assaults.

v.   **v. Web mining:** The event of World Wide net and its use develops, it'll stick with it manufacturing constantly content, structure, and utilization knowledge and also the estimation of net mining can continue increasing. analysis ought to be tired increase the correct set of net measurements, and their estimation techniques, extricating procedure models from utilization knowledge, seeing however distinctive components of the procedure model impact totally different net measurements of interest, and then forth.

vi.   **vi. Scientific Computing:** Analysis should be tired mining of alpha knowledge specifically approaches for mining cosmic, natural, synthetic, and liquid slashing knowledge analysis. The universal utilization of inserted systems in sleuthing and

48

activation environments plays major approaching developments in alpha process would force another category of techniques equipped for component knowledge analysis in defective, sent structure. The analysis in data processing needs a lot of thought in biological and environmental data analysis to use our native surround and resources.

vii. **vii. Business data:** Business data processing desires a lot of upgrades within the style of information mining techniques to extend important favorable circumstances in today's centered worldwide market place (E-Business). The info mining techniques hold impressive guarantees for growing new sets of tools which will be utilized to administer a lot of security to a typical man, increasing client satisfaction, giving best, protected and useful product at smart and stinting costs, in today's E-Business atmosphere.

In this means it will be seen that data processing has clothed to be a standout amongst the foremost ready tools in business. The framework taking under consideration data processing really beats the difficulty of prediction and analysis of choices that has brought impressive social and financial blessings. So, the info mining technology is popping resolute be a lot of powerful. Thorough knowledge warehouses that coordinate operational knowledge with client, supplier, and market data have caused a blast of data. Group action needs auspicious associated refined analysis on an incorporated perspective of the info. Be that because it could, there's a developing hole between all Thea lot of powerful storage and recovery systems and also the clients' capability to adequately investigate and follow abreast of the data they contain. Each relative and on-line Analytical process advances have prodigious skills for exploring monstrous knowledge warehouses, nonetheless animal power navigation of information is poor. Another innovative jump is predicted to structure and organize data for explicit end-client problems. The data mining tools will create this jump. Quantitative business blessings are incontestable through the mixing data mining together with information nodes and also the new product are coming back before long which will convey this integration to an excellent a lot of intensive gathering of individuals of consumers. We tend to found that data processing is popping resolute be increasingly regular in each the non-public and open sectors. Industrial enterprises, as an example, banking, insurance, solution, and marketing typically utilize data processing to decrease prices, improve analysis, and expand deals. On these lines, data processing are going to be a lot of valuable in future.

9. References

1. Priti Sharma and Smita, **Use of Data Mining in Different Fields,** Survey paper of Computer Science Engineering International Journal (May to June 2014).

2. Dr.C.Kumar Charliepaul. **Data Mining in Finance Sector,** International Journal of Engineering Sciences (July 2014).

3. Dr. K. Chitra **Data Mining Techniques- Its Applications in Banking Sector,** Interbational jounal of Emerging Technology and Advanced Engineering (August, 2013)

4. Ruxandra petre. **Data Mining Solutions To the people in the Business Environment,** article in University of Economic Studies, Romania (2013)

5. Abhijit A. Sawant (May, 2013). **Study of the different Data Mining Techniques used for Financial Data Assessment and Analysis.**

6. Chaoxiong Li. (October , 2012). **The Research and Implementation of Data Mining**

7. Neelamadhab Padhy. **Survey on Data Mining Applications and its Future Scope,** International Jouranl of Engineering and Information Technology(2012)

8. Abbas Keramati, Niloofar Wesfi, **A Proposed mechanism of Classification of Data Mining Techniques of the Credit Scoring,** International Journal of Industrial Engineering and Operations Management (2011)

www.ingramcontent.com/pod-product-compliance
Lightning Source LLC
La Vergne TN
LVHW042257060326
832902LV00009B/1103